BUILD THIS BONG

BUILD THIS BONG

Instructions and Diagrams for 40 Bongs, Pipes, and Hookahs

Text and illustrations by Randy Stratton

CHRONICLE BOOKS
SAN FRANCISCO

Text and illustration copyright
© 2007 by Randy Stratton.

All rights reserved. No part of this book may be
reproduced in any form without written permission
from the publisher.

Library of Congress Cataloging-in-Publication Data:
Stratton, Randy.

BUILD THIS BONG: Instructions And Diagrams
For 40 Bongs, Pipes, And Hookahs / text and
illustrations by Randy Stratton.
p. cm.

ISBN-13: 978-0-8118-5582-2
ISBN-10: 0-8118-5582-1

1. Handicraft. 2. Smoking paraphernalia. I. Title.
TT157.S826 2006
688'.4—dc22
2006012068

Manufactured in China
Designed by Samira Selod
Cover illustration by Jesse Ewing

Distributed in Canada
by Raincoast Books
9050 Shaughnessy Street
Vancouver, British Columbia V6P 6E5

10 9 8 7 6 5 4 3 2 1

Chronicle Books LLC
680 Second Street
San Francisco, California 94107
www.chroniclebooks.com

Krazy Straw is a registered trademark of Curt Products,
Inc. Plexiglas is a registered trademark of the Rohm
and Haas Company. Trademark owners do not sponsor,
endorse, or support the projects in Build This Bong.

A Disclaimer: This book is intended as a practical guide.
It is important that all the instructions are followed
carefully, as failure to do so could result in injury. Every
effort has been made to present the information in this
book in a clear, complete, and accurate manner. However,
not every situation can be anticipated and there can
be no substitute for common sense. As with any craft
project, check product labels to make sure the materials
you use are safe and nontoxic. The author and Chronicle '
Books disclaim any and all liability resulting from injuries
or damage caused during the production or use of the
crafts discussed in this book. It should go without saying
that smoking tobacco, wacky or otherwise, not only
"may be" but most definitely is hazardous to your health.
Further, neither Chronicle Books nor the author promotes
the use of illegal substances, and both parties hereby
disclaim any liability for any consequence of your choice
to use them in conjunction with the projects in this book.

The author would like to gratefully acknowledge his wife, his mother, and his editor. He would also like to thank all of those who helped with this project in any way, knowingly or otherwise, but who shall remain anonymous.

CONTENTS

INTRODUCTION

Despite the protestations of his body, man has long sought pleasure through the smoking of various plants and herbs. In an effort to increase his pleasure, he has also sought ways to increase the volume of smoke he may consume, while at the same time decreasing, through cooling and filtration, the discomforts associated with smoking. One such means is the use of a device commonly referred to as a *bong*.

Bongs have been around for ages, but it wasn't until the late '60s and early '70s that they were introduced to Western culture, by soldiers who had either seen or used similar devices while serving in Vietnam. There, simple pipes made from a section of bamboo, with a wooden bowl and stem and containing a small amount of water to cool and filter the smoke, are used for smoking raw tobacco. They are known as *thuoc lao* (pronounced "took-lau") pipes. The name *bhang* comes from the Thai language, and the word "bong" first appeared in Webster's dictionary in 1972. While the use of simple wooden water pipes for smoking tobacco is still widespread throughout Southeast Asia, modern bongs have evolved into a high-tech art form.

Modern bongs can be rather elaborate in their construction, but most bongs are still usually relatively simple. They will normally feature a small bowl attached to a stem, which is inserted into a cylinder that is usually partially filled with water. The bowl holds the material that is to be smoked, and will often hold only as much material as may be burned and inhaled in one deep breath. The stem connects the bowl to the cylinder, which will always have at least one open end from which to inhale the smoke.

A bong may also have a hole on the side of the chamber, above the level of the water, which is referred to as the *carb*—a term that is likely derived from the word *carburetor*. The use of a carb makes it easier to clear the chamber once it is filled with smoke. Some bongs may not have a carb hole, but rather an easily removable bowl—insulated in some way to prevent burning one's fingers—which allows the chamber to be cleared more easily as well. Hookahs may or may not have any sort of carb at all. A carb is not essential. It simply makes clearing the chamber of smoke quicker and easier.

Using a bong is quite easy. First, that which is going to be smoked is placed in the bowl, then the mouth is placed over the open end of the bong, and a finger is placed over the carb hole. Smoke is drawn into the bong as the contents of the bowl are burned. The smoke is cooled and filtered as it passes through the water. The remaining space within the cylinder allows for the expansion of the smoke. Once the bong is filled with smoke, the carb is released and the smoke is inhaled.

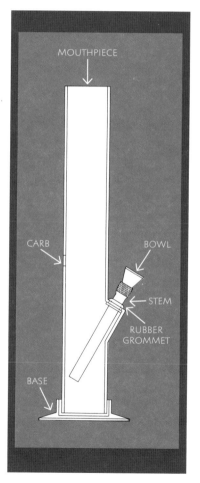

GETTING STARTED

The beauty of bongs is that they are such simple devices, they can be made from almost anything. Some basic tools are required, but no special skills are necessary. This book shows you how to make a variety of bongs. It also covers hookahs, which are similar to bongs but have a length of hose through which the smoke is inhaled, as well as a few pipes. The projects contained herein range from simple to elaborate, and use materials that may either be found around the house or easily obtained. Some are made entirely from items that can be found in the plumbing and lighting sections of your local hardware store, while others also require acrylic tubing and Plexiglas, which can be found at plastics specialty stores. Some are intended to work in a pinch and then be discarded after they have been used, while others are meant to last and even to be quite attractive.

One needn't be an experienced craftsperson to create completely functional smoking devices. The projects in this book are designed so that even if you're a novice, you will be able to build something that could not only pass for store-bought, but will likely impress your friends as well. Deciding which project to make will be less a matter of skill level, and more a matter of ambition and availability of supplies.

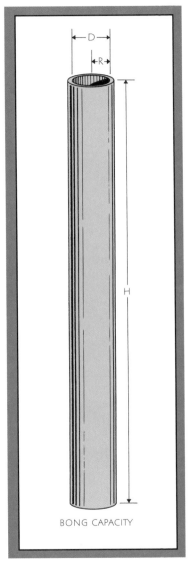

BONG CAPACITY

BONG CAPACITY

The projects in this book are designed to yield bongs, pipes, and hookahs of a given size. Keep in mind that these are simply guidelines. Feel free to make yours larger or smaller, if you like. Before doing so, however, it may be useful to know how much smoke your lungs can hold, and how to determine the volume of a bong or cylinder. Also, it is important to remember that a bong should not be so tall that you cannot reach the bowl to light it while your mouth is over the opening; otherwise you will need to have someone else light it for you.

Determining the volume of a cylinder is quite simple. First, multiply the square of its radius (the radius is half its diameter) by pi (3.14), then multiply the result by its height. To put it another way, radius $\times$ radius $\times$ pi $\times$ height $=$ volume. Or, $v = \pi r^2 h$.

For example:

A piece of acrylic tubing that is 18" long and has an inside diameter (ID) of 1¾" (1.75), or a radius of ⅞" (.875), will have a volume of about 43 cubic inches, because $.875 \times .875 \times 3.14 \times 18 = 43.27$.

To convert cubic inches to cubic centimeters, multiply inches by 16.39. So, $43.27 \times 16.39 = 709.20$, and 709.20 cubic centimeters is equal to about .71 liters.

LUNG CAPACITY

The average lung capacity of a normal human adult is between four and six liters, the equivalent of having two to three 2-liter beverage bottles in your chest cavity. A liter is exactly 1,000 cubic centimeters, or 61 cubic inches. Therefore, the average volume of a pair of human lungs is 4,000 to 6,000 cubic centimeters, or 244 to 366 cubic inches. However, the average amount of air taken into the lungs in a single breath is only about 0.5 liters (500 cubic centimeters), or 30.5 cubic inches. The amount of smoke you can inhale will depend on the sensitivity of your lungs, and will be somewhere between a normal breath and full capacity.

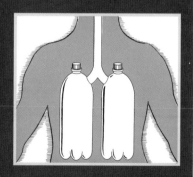

BONGS AND PIPES FROM MATERIALS FOUND AROUND THE HOUSE

It is said that necessity is the mother of invention, and this adage certainly holds true when one is in need of a bong or pipe. There is no need to leave the house for supplies. Even if you are on the go, a bong or pipe can be made quite easily from items at hand. An empty beverage container, paper-towel tube, or tampon applicator is a bong or pipe just waiting to happen. A bowl can be fashioned out of aluminum foil or carved out of a piece of produce, and a plastic pen tube will make an excellent stem. The beauty of such devices is that you can make them almost as quickly as you can discard them after they have done their duty. There are countless ways in which a bong or pipe can be made with items one might find lying around—the projects that follow are but a few examples.

BEVERAGE BOTTLE BONG

Materials and Supplies

One plastic pen

One small plastic bottle, such as a 16-ounce or 1-liter beverage bottle

Aluminum foil

Tools

X-Acto knife, or similar sharp, pointy instrument

Directions

• Remove the contents of the pen so that all that remains is the empty plastic tube.

• Place either the tip of your finger or the cap from the bottle against the end of the pen tube, and wrap a strip of foil a few inches wide around the area where the two meet, then squeeze the foil so that it is snug against them. Then remove your finger or the bottle cap to reveal a bowl-shaped piece of foil.

• Take a square of foil a couple of layers thick and work it into the bowl-shaped piece of foil, then fold the edges down around the outside of the bowl. Poke a few small holes in the bottom of the bowl to create a screen, then slide the tin-foil bowl up the plastic pen tube a little to avoid melting it when the bowl is lit. This may take some practice.

• Using the knife, cut two holes on opposite sides of the plastic bottle. Make sure that the holes are as smooth and circular as possible, and that at least one of the holes is just slightly smaller than the outside diameter of the pen tube so that it fits tightly. This will help prevent leaks.

• Insert the other end of the pen tube into the hole in the plastic bottle, angling it toward the bottom. Add enough water so that the bottom of the stem is submerged, but not so much that there is a risk of water leaking out of either the bowl or the hole through which the stem passes.

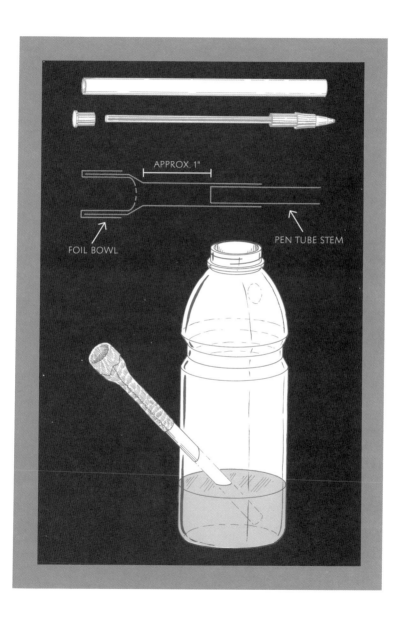

APPROX. 1"

FOIL BOWL

PEN TUBE STEM

STEAMROLLER

Materials and Supplies

One cardboard paper-towel tube

Aluminum foil

Tools

X-Acto knife, or similar sharp, pointy instrument

Directions

• Using the knife, cut a 1" hole a few inches from one end of the paper-towel tube.

• Cut a strip of aluminum foil approximately 3" wide and 12" long. Wrap the aluminum foil around the tube, completely covering the hole. Gently work the foil into the hole to create a bowl. This may take some practice, as the aluminum foil can tear easily.

• Using the knife, carefully poke a few small holes in the bowl to create a screen.

• Cover the end of the tube with one hand when lighting the bowl. Remove hand when the tube is full to release the smoke.

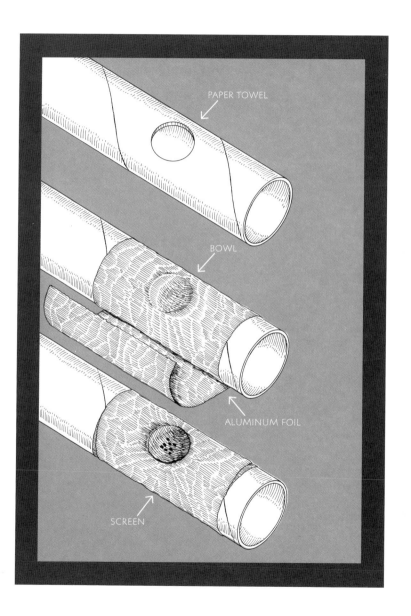

PAPER TOWEL

BOWL

ALUMINUM FOIL

SCREEN

17

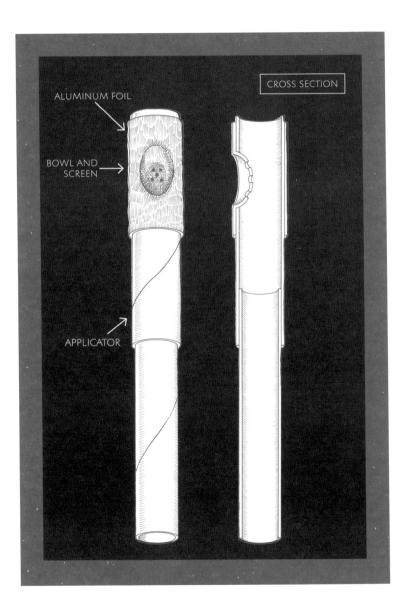

CROSS SECTION

ALUMINUM FOIL

BOWL AND
SCREEN

APPLICATOR

TAM-PIPE

Materials and Supplies

One tampon with a cardboard applicator

Aluminum foil

Tools

X-Acto knife, or similar sharp, pointy instrument

Directions

• Remove the tampon from the applicator and discard.

• Using the knife, cut a ½" hole approximately ½" from the end of the larger half of the applicator.

• Cut a strip of aluminum foil approximately 1½" wide and 6" long. Wrap the aluminum foil around the applicator, completely covering the hole. Gently work the foil into the hole to create a bowl. This may take some practice, as the aluminum foil can tear easily.

• Using the knife, carefully poke a few small holes in the bowl to create a screen.

• Place a finger over the end of the tampon when lighting the bowl. Remove finger to release the smoke.

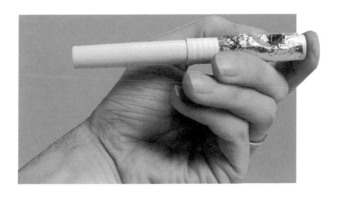

CANTALOUPE BONG

Materials and Supplies

One cantaloupe

Toothpicks

Tools

Knife

Ice pick, chopstick, or similar tool

Directions

• Lay the cantaloupe on its side and cut off the top one-third of the melon, just above the dimple on one end.

• Scoop out the seeds from the inside of the cantaloupe and discard them.

• In one end of the larger part of the cantaloupe, carve a small cone-shaped bowl just below the rim. Using an ice pick, chopstick, or similar tool, poke a hole from the bottom of the bowl through to the inside of the cantaloupe. Angle the hole toward the bottom of the cavity.

• With the knife, cut two holes about ½" in diameter in the lid of the cantaloupe — one toward the front (closer to the bowl) for the carb, and one toward the back for the mouthpiece.

• Before using, fill the cantaloupe with water to just below the level of the bowl, and replace the lid. Insert toothpicks to hold the lid in place.

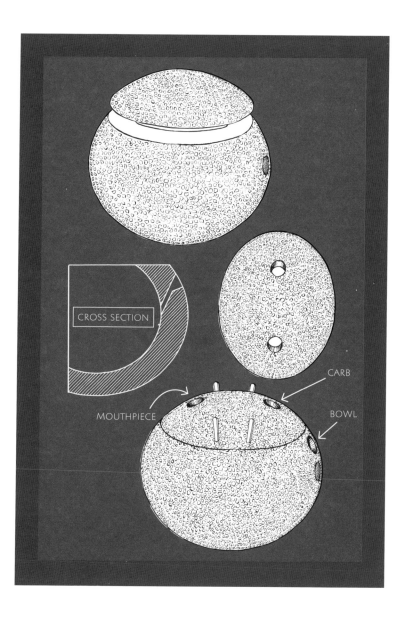

CROSS SECTION

CARB

MOUTHPIECE

BOWL

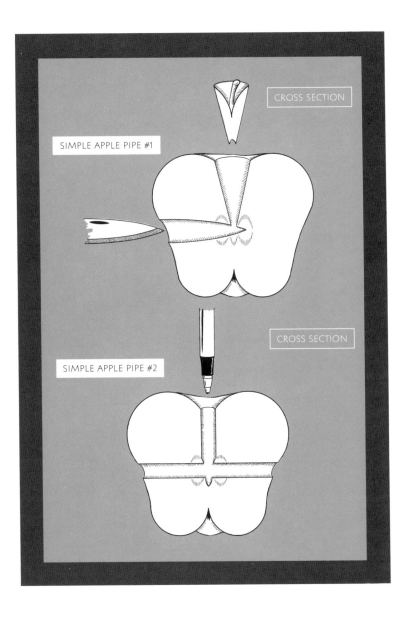

CROSS SECTION

SIMPLE APPLE PIPE #1

CROSS SECTION

SIMPLE APPLE PIPE #2

SIMPLE APPLE PIPES

Simple Apple Pipe #1

Materials and Supplies

One apple

Tools

Small knife

Directions

• Using the knife, carve a cone-shaped bowl from the top of the apple to the center of the core.

• Carve another small hole in one side of the apple that just barely connects with the bowl.

Simple Apple Pipe #2

Materials and Supplies

One apple

Tools

Plastic pen

Directions

• Push the pen through the apple so there is a hole from one side of the apple to the other. The core will be tough to penetrate, so you may have to push the pen in from each side toward the core. The opening on one side will serve as a mouthpiece; the other will serve as a carb.

• To create the bowl, remove the apple stem and push the tip of the pen into the indentation in the top of the apple toward the core so that it connects with the first hole, being careful not to push the pen out the bottom of the apple.

elaborate **APPLE PIPE**

Materials and Supplies

One apple

Plastic pen

Aluminum foil

Tools

Knife

Directions

• Using the knife, carve a cone-shaped bowl from the top of the apple to the center of the core.

• Push the pen through the apple so there is a hole from one side of the apple to the other. The core will be tough to penetrate, so you may have to push the pen in from each side toward the core.

• Remove the contents of the pen so that all that remains is an empty plastic tube. Insert the pen tube into one of the holes in the side of the apple. This will be used for a mouthpiece. The other end of the hole, in the other side of the apple, will serve as a carb.

• Make a small square of aluminum foil that is a couple of layers thick. Using the knife, poke a few small holes in the center of the foil square. Place one finger in the center of the square, and form the foil around it to create a bowl. Insert the foil into the hole in the top of the apple, folding the edges of the foil down around the outside of the apple.

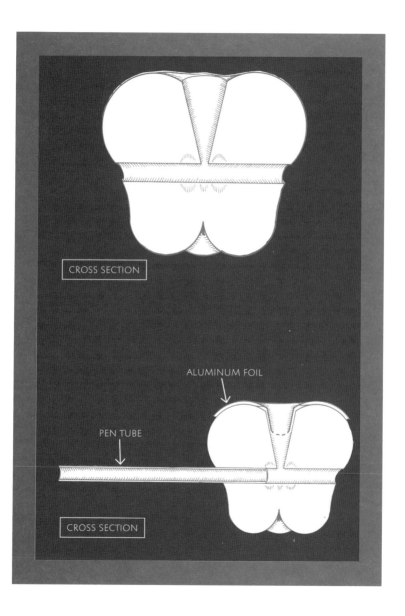

CROSS SECTION

ALUMINUM FOIL

PEN TUBE

CROSS SECTION

25

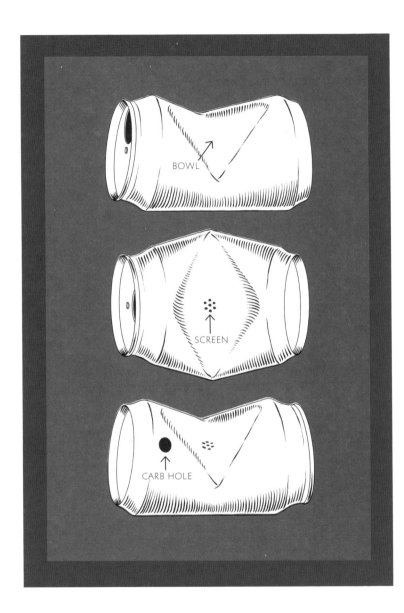

ALUMINUM CAN PIPE

Materials and Supplies

One empty aluminum can

Tools

Knife

Directions

• Remove the tab from the top of the can.

• Make a deep indentation in the side of the can to create a bowl. Using the knife, poke a few small holes in the indentation to create a screen.

• Cut a hole in the side of the can for a carb.

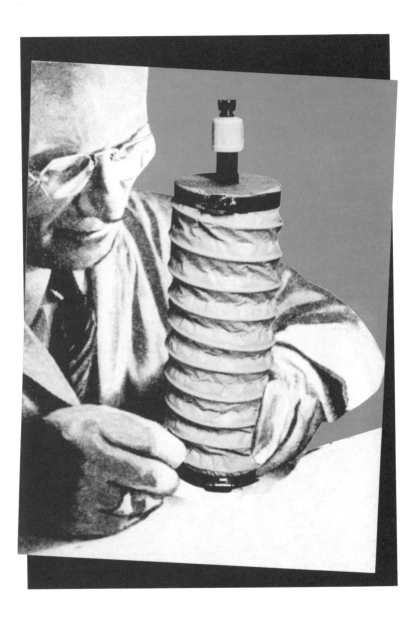

Bongs, Pipes, and Hookahs From Common Hardware Store Items

Perfectly serviceable and durable bongs, pipes, and hookahs can be made from just a handful of items found in the plumbing and lighting sections of a decent hardware store. Such items also can be found at plumbers' supply stores and stores that specialize in lamps and lighting. Plumbing hardware may appear somewhat crude, whereas a number of pieces of lamp hardware are identical to pieces you find on store-bought smoking devices. For example, the pieces that are used to make the bowls found on most pipes are actually referred to in the hardware industry as "cut nozzles." Most plumbing hardware may be used in conjunction with lamp hardware, and by combining the two you can build just about anything. The possibilities are virtually endless.

The projects in this section call for the simplest approach and the most easily obtainable materials and supplies, but feel free to experiment. There may be times when you'll want to, or have to, make substitutions. In some cases, it may be necessary to make minor adjustments, such as drilling a larger or smaller hole when using larger or smaller parts. A good fit is important, and should be considered before beginning a project.

This section begins with a few simple pipes just to get you started. These are the simplest projects because they don't require any tools at all. Making them will show you just how easy it can be to put something together once you know what you are looking for and have gathered a few supplies.

FOUR PIPES

Pipe #1

Materials and Supplies

One ⅜" or ¼" F × ⅛" M brass cut nozzle

One 3" × ⅛" M brass nipple

One ⅛" F × ⅛" F 90-degree-angle brass pipe elbow

One ⅛" F brass pyramid knob with a hole for a beaded chain

Screen (an aerator screen cut to fit the bowl, or an appropriately sized screen purchased from a smoke shop)

Directions

• Thread the cut nozzle and the nipple into either side of the elbow, and thread the pyramid knob onto the other end of the nipple. Insert the screen into the bowl.

Pipe #2

Materials and Supplies

One ⅜" or ¼" F × ⅛" M brass cut nozzle

One ⅛" F × ⅛" M 90-degree-angle brass pipe elbow

One ⅛" F brass coupler

One ⅛" F brass pyramid knob with a hole for a beaded chain

One 3" × ⅛" M brass nipple

Screen (an aerator screen cut to fit the bowl, or an appropriately sized screen purchased from a smoke shop)

Directions

• Thread the cut nozzle into the female side of the 90-degree-angle elbow, and thread the male side of the 90-degree-angle elbow into one end of the coupler. Thread the pyramid knob onto the nipple, and thread the nipple into the other end of the coupler. Insert the screen into the bowl.

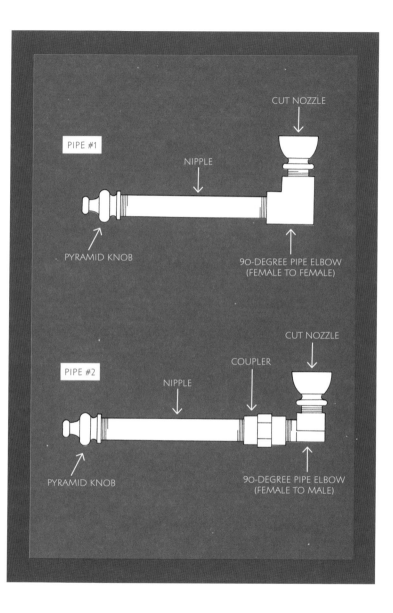

PIPE #1

CUT NOZZLE

NIPPLE

PYRAMID KNOB

90-DEGREE PIPE ELBOW
(FEMALE TO FEMALE)

PIPE #2

CUT NOZZLE

COUPLER

NIPPLE

PYRAMID KNOB

90-DEGREE PIPE ELBOW
(FEMALE TO MALE)

31

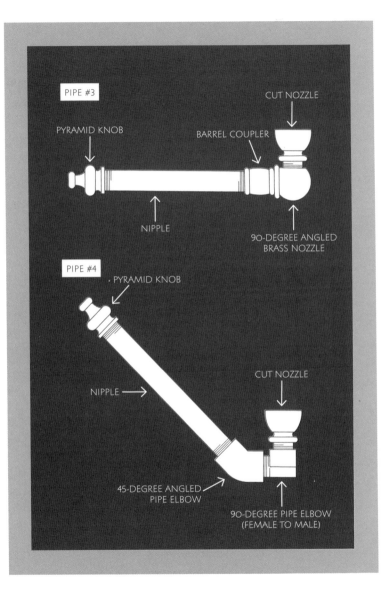

PIPE #3

PYRAMID KNOB

CUT NOZZLE

BARREL COUPLER

NIPPLE

90-DEGREE ANGLED
BRASS NOZZLE

PIPE #4

PYRAMID KNOB

CUT NOZZLE

NIPPLE

45-DEGREE ANGLED
PIPE ELBOW

90-DEGREE PIPE ELBOW
(FEMALE TO MALE)

Pipe #3

Materials and Supplies

One ⅜" or ¼" F × ⅛" M brass cut nozzle

One ⅛" F × ⅛" M 90-degree-angle brass nozzle

⅛" F brass barrel coupler

One ⅛" F brass pyramid knob with a hole for a beaded chain

One 3" × ⅛" M brass nipple

Screen (an aerator screen cut to fit the bowl, or an appropriately sized screen purchased from a smoke shop)

Directions

• Thread the cut nozzle into the female side of the angled nozzle and thread the barrel coupler onto the male side. Thread the pyramid knob onto the nipple, and thread the nipple into the coupler. Insert the screen into the bowl.

Pipe #4

Materials and Supplies

One ⅜" or ¼" F × ⅛" M brass cut nozzle

One ⅛" F × ⅛" M 90-degree-angle brass pipe elbow

One ⅛" F × ⅛" F 45-degree-angle brass pipe elbow

One ⅛" F brass pyramid knob with a hole for a beaded chain

One 3" × ⅛" M brass nipple

Screen (an aerator screen cut to fit the bowl, or an appropriately sized screen purchased from a smoke shop)

Directions

• Thread the cut nozzle into the female side of the 90-degree-angle elbow, and thread the male side of the 90-degree-angle elbow into one end of the 45-degree-angle elbow. Thread the pyramid knob onto the nipple, and thread the nipple into the other end of the 45-degree-angle elbow. Insert the screen into the bowl.

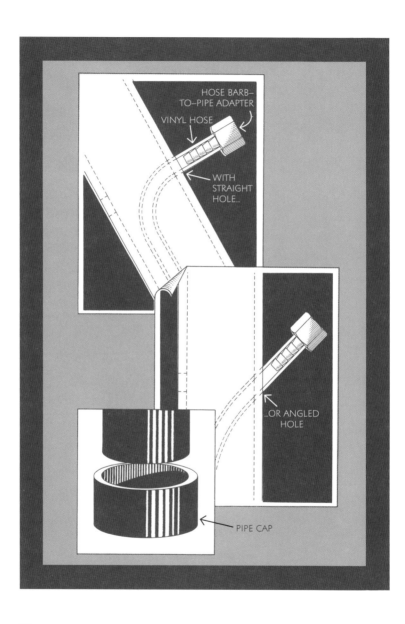

HOSE BARB–
TO–PIPE ADAPTER

VINYL HOSE

WITH
STRAIGHT
HOLE...

...OR ANGLED
HOLE

PIPE CAP

Basic PIPE BONG

Materials and Supplies

One 18" length of 1½" ID ABS or PVC pipe

One ¼" HB × ¼" F brass hose barb–to–pipe adapter

One 5" length of ¼" ID × ⅜" OD flexible vinyl hose

Screen (an aerator screen cut to fit the bowl, or an appropriately sized screen purchased from a smoke shop)

One 1½" pipe cap

Tools

Drill and ⅜" drill bit

Sandpaper

Directions

• Drill two ⅜" holes on opposite sides of the pipe approximately 6" up from the bottom end. (Angling one of the holes downward for the stem and bowl may be desirable, but is not necessary. Drilling a shallow starter hole with a smaller drill bit first will make drilling at an angle a little easier.)

• Sand the ends of the pipe smooth.

• Insert the hose barb, which is the bowl, into the vinyl hose, which is the stem. Insert the hose into the pipe, angling the hose toward the bottom of the pipe. Insert the screen into the bowl.

• Place the pipe cap on the bottom end of the pipe.

PLUNGER BONG

Materials and Supplies

One 24" length of 1½" ID ABS or PVC pipe

One 1½" wye-joint

Two 1½" pipe caps

One ¼" HB × ¼" F brass hose barb–to–pipe adapter

One 8" length of ¼" ID × ⅜" OD flexible vinyl hose

Screen (an aerator screen cut to fit the bowl, or an appropriately sized screen purchased from a smoke shop)

Tools

Drill and ⅜" drill bit

Sandpaper

Directions

• Cut the pipe into two pieces 2" long, and one piece 20" long.

• Sand the ends of the pieces of pipe smooth.

• Insert the long piece of pipe into the top of the wye-joint. Insert the two 2" pieces snugly into the bottom and side of the wye-joint, and place one of the pipe caps snugly on the short piece of pipe on the bottom of the wye-joint.

• Drill a ⅜" hole in the center of the other pipe cap.

• Insert the hose barb, which is the bowl, into the hose, which is the stem. Insert the screen into the bowl. Insert the hose into the hole in the cap, and place the cap on the short piece of pipe on the side of the wye-joint. Do not put the cap on so tightly that it is difficult to remove.

Note: This bong doesn't have a regular carb. To use, remove the cap with the bowl and stem once the chamber is filled to release the smoke.

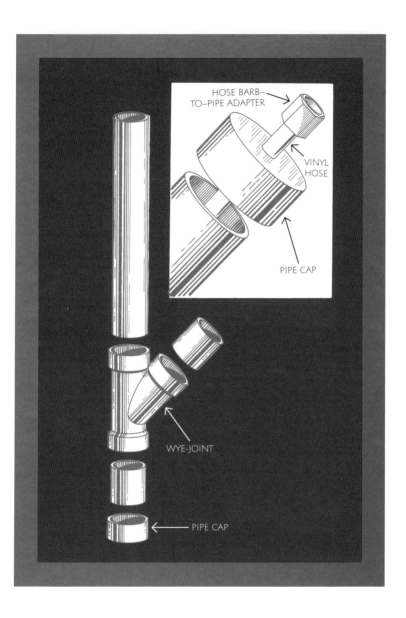

HOSE BARB–
TO–PIPE ADAPTER

VINYL
HOSE

PIPE CAP

WYE-JOINT

PIPE CAP

BUCKET BONG

Materials and Supplies

One large plastic bottle, such as a 2-liter beverage bottle

One ⅜" or ¼" F × ⅛" M brass cut nozzle

Screen (an aerator screen cut to fit the bowl, or an appropriately sized screen purchased from a smoke shop)

One large bucket or other container filled with water

Tools

X-Acto knife, or similar sharp, pointy instrument

Drill and ⅜" drill bit (optional)

Directions

• Cut off the bottom of the bottle with the knife.

• Drill or cut a ⅜" hole in the beverage bottle cap.

• Thread the cut nozzle into the hole on the outside of the cap, and screw the cap onto the bottle. Insert the screen into the bowl.

Note: To use, immerse the bottle up to its neck in water. Be sure to load the bowl after *the bottle has been immersed. Then, while lighting the bowl, slowly lift the bottle until the bottom is just below the surface of the water. Hold the bong in place while removing the cap. Push the bong down to release the smoke through the beverage bottle opening.*

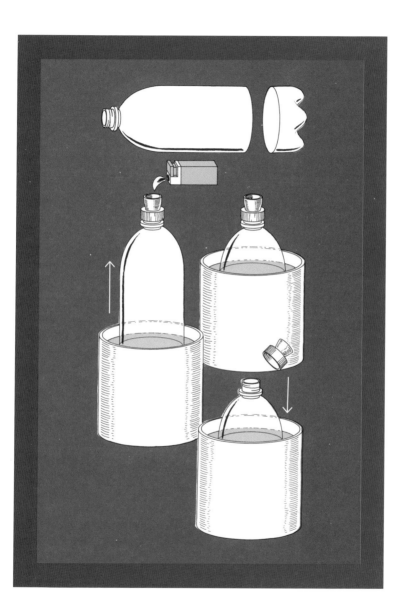

BOWL

RUBBER STOPPER

WATERFALL BONG

Materials and Supplies

One large plastic bottle, such as a 2-liter beverage bottle

One 1" rubber sink stopper

One ⅜" or ¼" F × ⅛" M brass cut nozzle

Screen (an aerator screen cut to fit the bowl, or an appropriately sized screen purchased from a smoke shop)

Tools

X-Acto knife, or similar sharp, pointy instrument

Drill and ⅜" drill bit (optional)

Directions

• Cut a 1" hole near the bottom of the bottle and insert the rubber stopper. (Cutting the hole as smooth and round as possible will help prevent leakage.)

• Drill or cut a ⅜" hole in the lid of the beverage bottle.

• Thread the cut nozzle into the hole on the outside of the cap. Insert the screen into the bowl.

Note: To use, fill the bottle up to its neck with water, and screw the lid onto the bottle. Load the bowl, then pull out the stopper and light the bowl as the water drains out. As the water drains out, it will draw smoke into the bottle. Remove the cap after the water has drained out to release the smoke.

DRYER HOSE SUCTION BONG

Materials and Supplies

One 12" length of 1" × 6" pine wood, or similar

One 12" length of 4" diameter flexible plastic dryer hose

Two 4" adjustable hose clamps

One ½" × 2" PVC nipple

One ½" PVC threaded cap

One ⅜" or ¼" F × ⅛" M brass cut nozzle

One ⅛" thin brass hex nut, if needed

Screen (an aerator screen cut to fit the bowl, or an appropriately sized screen purchased from a smoke shop)

Tools

Jigsaw

Drill, and ¹³/₁₆" boring bit, and ⅜" drill bit

Directions

• Cut two 4" circles of wood with the jigsaw, and drill a ¹³/₁₆" hole in the center of one of the pieces.

• Insert the pieces of wood into the ends of the dryer hose, and secure them with the hose clamps.

• Thread the nipple into the hole in the piece of wood.

• Drill a ⅜" hole in the threaded cap, and thread the cut nozzle into the outside of the cap. Thread a hex nut onto the cut nozzle on the inside of the cap if necessary to secure the nozzle to the cap, and thread the cap onto the nipple. Insert the screen into the bowl.

Note: To use, compress the dryer hose, then load the bowl. Light the bowl while slowly extending the hose. Remove the cap, and compress the hose to release the smoke.

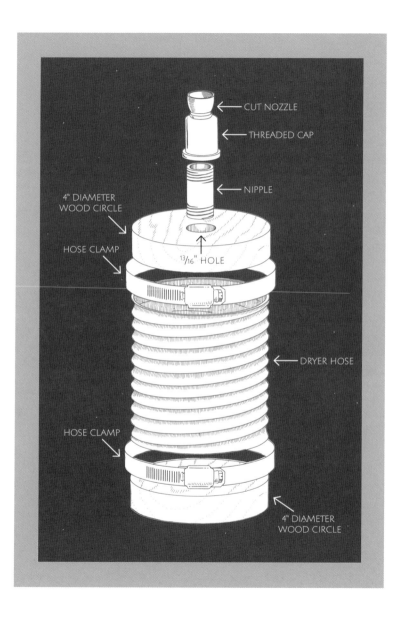

CUT NOZZLE

THREADED CAP

NIPPLE

4" DIAMETER WOOD CIRCLE

HOSE CLAMP

13/16" HOLE

DRYER HOSE

HOSE CLAMP

4" DIAMETER WOOD CIRCLE

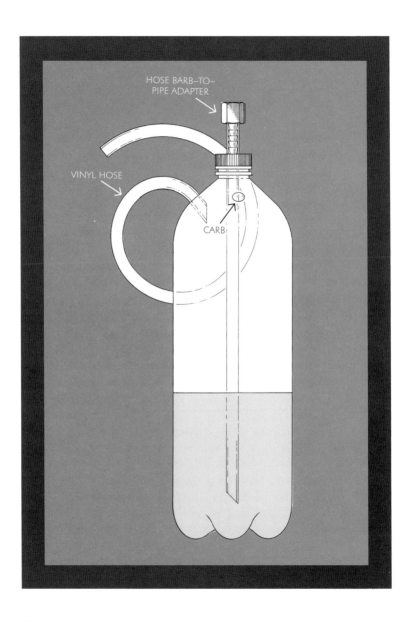

HOSE BARB-TO-
PIPE ADAPTER

VINYL HOSE

CARB

One-Person
BEVERAGE BOTTLE HOOKAH

Materials and Supplies

One plastic bottle, such as a 2-liter beverage bottle

Approximately 2' of ¼" ID × ⅜" OD flexible vinyl hose

One ¼" HB × ¼" F brass hose barb–to–pipe adapter

Screen (an aerator screen cut to fit the bowl, or an appropriately sized screen purchased from a smoke shop)

Tools

X-Acto knife, or similar sharp, pointy instrument

Drill and ⅜" drill bit (optional)

Directions

• Cut or drill two ⅜" holes in the side of the bottle near the neck. Be sure to make at least one of the holes as smooth and round as possible, and just slightly smaller than the outside diameter of the hose to avoid leakage.

• Cut or drill a ⅜" hole in the bottle cap.

• Cut one piece of hose slightly shorter than the height of the bottle, angling the cut at one end. (The angle will make it easier to insert the hose later.) Insert the hose barb, which is the bowl, into the straight end of the measured length of hose, which is the stem, and insert the angled end of the hose into the lid. Insert the screen into the bowl.

• Insert the angled end of the remaining hose about ½" into one of the holes in the side of the bottle, fill the bottle halfway with water, and screw the cap onto the bottle.

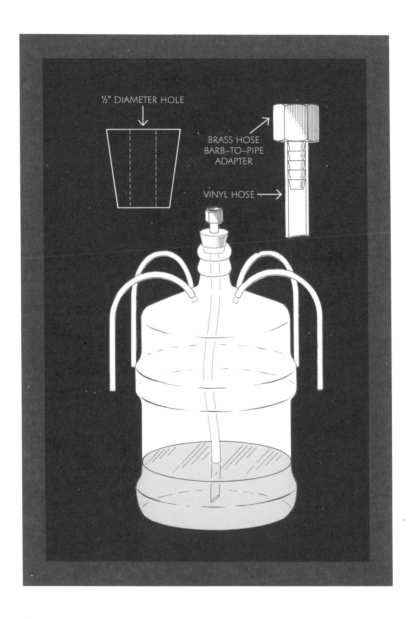

½" DIAMETER HOLE

BRASS HOSE BARB–TO–PIPE ADAPTER

VINYL HOSE

Four-Person
BEVERAGE BOTTLE HOOKAH

Materials and Supplies

One large plastic bottle, such as a 5-gallon water bottle

One large cork or stopper (sized to fit the mouth of the bottle)

Approximately 8' of ⅜" ID × ½" OD flexible vinyl hose

One ⅜" HB × ½" F brass hose barb–to–pipe adapter

Screen (an aerator screen cut to fit the bowl, or an appropriately sized screen purchased from a smoke shop)

Tools

Drill and ½" drill bit

Directions

• Drill five ½" holes in the side of the bottle near the neck.

• Drill a ½" hole in the cork or stopper.

• Cut one piece of hose slightly shorter than the height of the bottle, angling the cut at one end. (The angle will make it easier to insert the hose later.) Insert the hose barb, which is the bowl, into the straight end of the measured length of hose, which is the stem, and insert the angled end of the hose into the cork or stopper. Insert the screen into the bowl.

• Cut the remaining piece of hose into four equal lengths, each with one angled and one straight end. Insert the angled ends of the four hoses about ½" into four of the holes in the side of the bottle. Fill the bottle halfway with water, and insert the cork or stopper with the bowl and stem into the mouth of the bottle.

ANY-BOTTLE
HOOKAH ATTACHMENT

Materials and Supplies

One rubber stopper, or cork (size may vary)

One 12" piece of ¼" OD round brass tubing

One ¼" COMP × ⅜" F brass compression nut–to–pipe adapter

Screen (an aerator screen cut to fit the bowl, or an appropriately sized screen purchased from a smoke shop)

One 12" length of ⅛" ID × ¼" OD flexible vinyl hose

Tools

Drill

Wrench

Directions

• Drill two ¼" holes in the stopper by cutting off a 4" length of the brass tubing and inserting it into the drill and using it as a bit.

• Slide the compression nut and sleeve onto the end of the remaining piece of brass tubing, and insert the tube into the compression fitting until it reaches the end. Tighten the compression nut onto the compression fitting with the wrench. Insert the screen into the bowl.

• Insert the brass tubing and compression fitting all the way into one of the holes in the larger end of the stopper, and insert the vinyl hose into the other hole until it just clears the other side of the stopper.

• This attachment may be used with any bottle that has an opening in which the rubber stopper or cork will fit snugly.

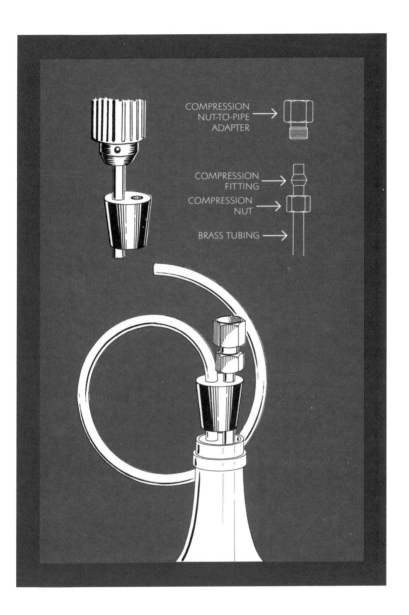

COMPRESSION
NUT-TO-PIPE
ADAPTER

COMPRESSION
FITTING

COMPRESSION
NUT

BRASS TUBING

FROZEN HOOKAH

Materials and Supplies

One 3' length of ¼" ID × ⅜" OD flexible vinyl hose

One large drinking glass, such as a pint glass

One ¼" HB × ¼" F brass hose barb–to–pipe adapter

Screen (an aerator screen cut to fit the bowl, or an appropriately sized screen purchased from a smoke shop)

Directions

• Coil the vinyl hose around the inside of the drinking glass, leaving a few inches of either end above the rim of the glass. One end will be the mouthpiece, and the other will be the stem for the bowl.

• Insert the hose barb into one end of the hose for the bowl, and insert the screen into the bowl.

• Fill the glass about two-thirds full of water, and place it in the freezer to prepare it for use.

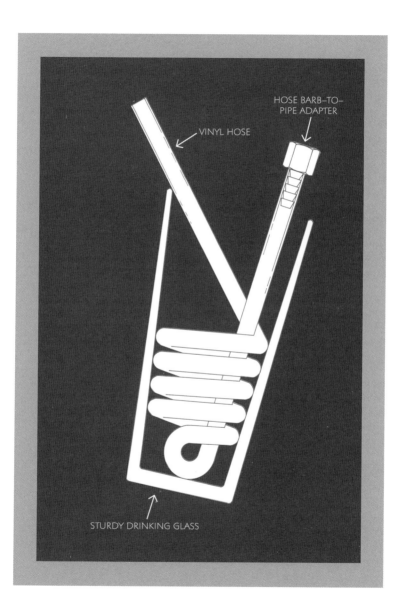

HOSE BARB–TO–
PIPE ADAPTER

VINYL HOSE

STURDY DRINKING GLASS

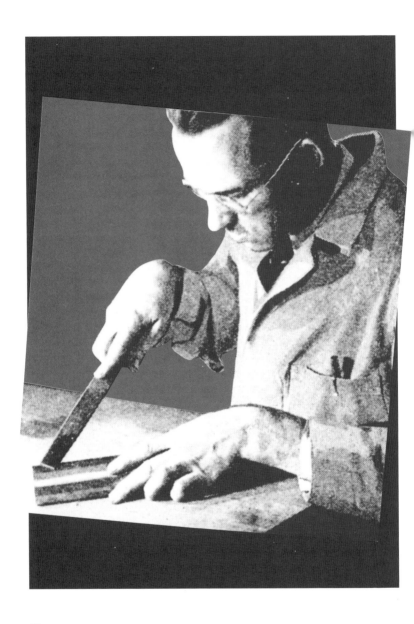

Bongs and Hookahs Made From

ACRYLIC TUBING AND PLEXIGLAS

Most store-bought bongs are made from pieces of clear acrylic tubing and sheets of plastic commonly referred to as Plexiglas. You can find similar materials at stores that specialize in plastics, and they're available in a wide variety of colors and sizes. Acrylic tubing is usually sold in lengths of four feet or longer, which will yield several bongs, and most stores will sell small pieces of scrap Plexiglas. It is easier than you might think to build bongs, hookahs, and pipes with acrylic tubing and Plexiglas and just a few special tools.

When it comes to cutting, almost anything that will cut wood will work fine on acrylic tubing or Plexiglas. Carpenter's saws, miter saws, jigsaws, circular saws, and band saws are just a few options.

When cutting thinner material, such as ⅛"-thick sheets of Plexiglas, a scoring tool will also work well.

Drilling acrylic tubing or Plexiglas is a little tougher than cutting it, though. Acrylic tubing and Plexiglas are more brittle than wood, and will crack if you don't drill carefully. Drill bits with either a 60-degree angled tip or what is referred to as a "bullet point" will minimize the risk of cracking.

If these are not available, standard drill bits will work so long as the hole is started with a smaller drill bit and enlarged incrementally using successively larger bits until the desired size is achieved. This method may sometimes be necessary even when a specialized bit is available. It is always a good idea to practice cutting and drilling on a piece of scrap first.

You can also find adhesives specifically formulated for use with acrylic tubing and Plexiglas, which are generally referred to as acrylic cement. Acrylic cement usually comes in both regular (thin) and thickened versions. A thicker adhesive will be easier to use because it is less likely to run. It is always best to use the appropriate adhesive whenever possible. When acrylic cement is not available, plastic model cement, silicone caulk, or some epoxies may work in certain situations. Always read and follow the instructions on the product package, and experiment on scrap pieces!

It's worth mentioning a primary difference between manufactured bongs and bongs you can make yourself. Most manufactured bongs are made using a process called vacuum-forming, in which plastic is heated and then molded into various shapes using vacuum pressure. This is what allows the stem and bowl to be inserted into a bong at an angle. Vacuum forming requires special equipment, and goes a little beyond what the average person will be able to do in their home or workshop. The projects in the following sections address this problem through various means.

In this section you will find projects that range from simple to elaborate, representing just a few of the possibilities. There are an almost infinite number of ways to put together a few feet of tubing, some Plexiglas, and maybe a length of flexible vinyl hose. You may be surprised by how easy it is—once you are familiar with the materials—to make something that is both clever and unique all on your own! These projects also serve as a good introduction to the world of plastics.

Basic ACRYLIC BONG

Materials and Supplies

One 12" length of 2" OD × 1¾" ID acrylic tubing

One ⅜" or ¼" F × ⅛" M brass cut nozzle

One ⅛" F × ⅛" M 45-degree-angle brass nozzle

One 5" length of ⅜" ID × ½" OD flexible vinyl hose

Screen (an aerator screen cut to fit the bowl, or an appropriately sized screen purchased from a smoke shop)

One 2" ID polyethylene cap, or one 4" × 4" piece of ⅛"-thick Plexiglas

Acrylic cement, if using Plexiglas

Tools

Drill and ½" drill bit (with a 60-degree or bullet-point tip)

Sandpaper

Directions

• Drill two ½" holes on opposite sides of the acrylic tubing approximately 4" up from the bottom end.

• Sand the ends of the acrylic tubing smooth.

• Thread the cut nozzle into the angled nozzle, and thread the angled nozzle into the vinyl hose. Insert the vinyl hose through one of the holes in the outside of the pipe, angling the hose toward the bottom of the pipe. Insert the screen into the bowl.

• Place the polyethylene cap on the bottom of the acrylic tubing, or attach the acrylic tubing to the piece of Plexiglas with acrylic cement.

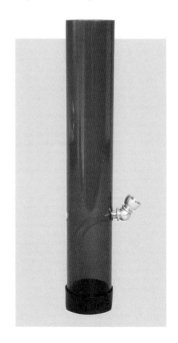

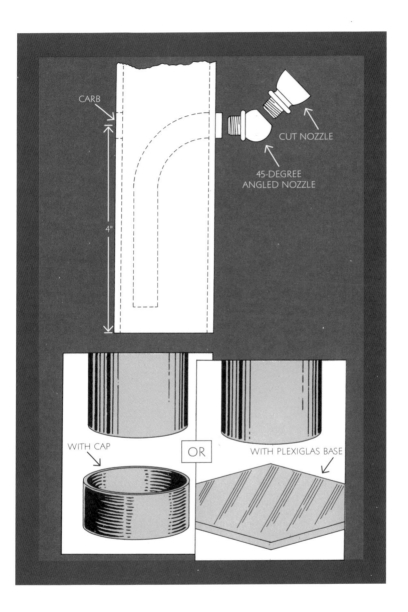

CARB

CUT NOZZLE

45-DEGREE
ANGLED NOZZLE

4"

WITH CAP

OR

WITH PLEXIGLAS BASE

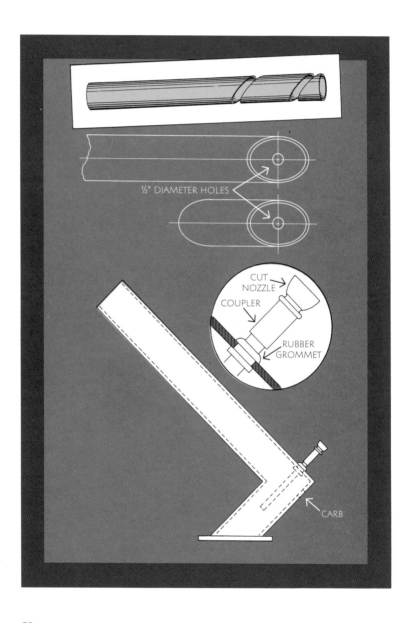

½" DIAMETER HOLES

CUT NOZZLE

COUPLER

RUBBER GROMMET

CARB

58

PISTOL-GRIP BONG

Materials and Supplies

One 18" length of 2" OD × 1¾" ID acrylic tubing

Acrylic cement

One 4" × 4" piece of ⅜"-thick Plexiglas

One ⅜" or ¼" F × ⅛" M brass cut nozzle

One ⅛" F brass coupler

One 4" × ⅛" M brass nipple

One ⅜" ID × ⅝" OD rubber grommet

Screen (an aerator screen cut to fit the bowl, or an appropriately sized screen purchased from a smoke shop)

Tools

Drill and ½" drill bit (with a 60-degree or bullet-point tip)

Sandpaper

Directions

• Cut one piece of acrylic tubing approximately 14" long (overall length), with a 45-degree-angle on one end. Cut both ends of the remaining piece at 45 degrees, so that it has a mean length of about 4".

• Drill a ½" hole about 1" in from the angled end of the long piece of tubing for the stem and bowl, and drill a ½" hole about 1" in from one end of the short piece of tubing for the carb.

• Sand all ends of the acrylic tubing smooth.

• Cement the two ends of the tubing with holes in them together at a right angle, and cement the short piece onto the Plexiglas base.

• Thread the cut nozzle into the coupler, and thread the coupler onto the nipple. Insert the grommet into the hole in the longer piece of acrylic tubing, and insert the nipple into the grommet. Insert the screen into the bowl.

ACRYLIC HOOKAH

Materials and Supplies

One 6" length of 2" OD × 1¾" ID acrylic tubing

One 4" × 4" piece of ⅛" thick Plexiglas

Acrylic cement

One 2" ID polyethylene cap

Two ⅜" ID × ⅝" OD rubber grommets

One ⅜" or ¼" F × ⅛" M brass cut nozzle

One ⅛" F brass coupler

One 5" × ⅛" M brass nipple

Screen (an aerator screen cut to fit the bowl, or an appropriately sized screen purchased from a smoke shop)

One 12" length of ¼" ID × ⅜" OD flexible vinyl hose

One ⅛" F brass pyramid knob with a hole for a beaded chain (optional)

Tools

Drill and ½" drill bit (with a 60-degree or bullet-point tip)

Sandpaper

Directions

• Drill one ½" hole in the acrylic tubing about 1¼" down from the top.

• Sand the ends of the acrylic tubing smooth and attach it to the piece of Plexiglas with acrylic cement.

• Drill two ½" holes in the polyethylene cap, and insert the rubber grommets into the holes.

• Thread the cut nozzle into the coupler, thread the coupler onto the nipple, and insert the nipple into one of the grommets in the polyethylene cap. Insert the screen into the bowl.

• Insert one end of the vinyl hose about ½" into the other grommet, and thread the pyramid knob (if using) onto the other end of the hose.

• Fill the acrylic tube two-thirds full with water before placing the cap on the tube.

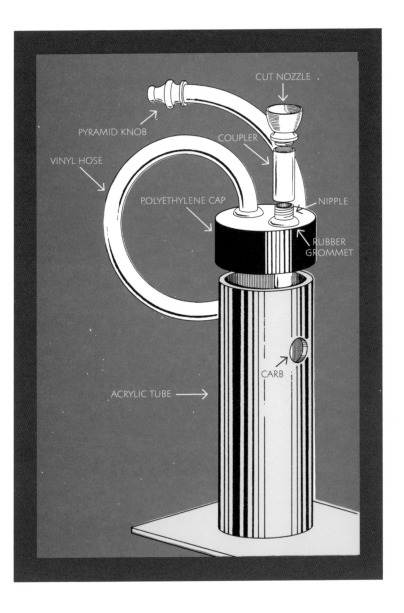

CUT NOZZLE

PYRAMID KNOB

COUPLER

VINYL HOSE

NIPPLE

POLYETHYLENE CAP

RUBBER GROMMET

CARB

ACRYLIC TUBE

HORIZONTAL HOOKAH

Materials and Supplies

One 6" length of 2" OD × 1¾" ID acrylic tubing

Two 3" × 3" pieces of ⅛"-thick Plexiglas

Acrylic cement

Two ⅜" ID × ⅝" OD rubber grommets

One ⅜" or ¼" F × ⅛" M brass cut nozzle

One ⅛" F brass coupler

One 2" × ⅛" M brass nipple

Screen (an aerator screen cut to fit the bowl, or an appropriately sized screen purchased from a smoke shop)

One 12" length of ¼" ID × ⅜" OD flexible vinyl hose

One ⅛" F brass pyramid knob with a hole for a beaded chain (optional)

One 1" rubber stopper

Tools

Drill and ½" drill bit (with a 60-degree or bullet-point tip)

1" boring bit

Sandpaper

Directions

• Drill three ½" holes spaced about 1½" apart along one side of the acrylic tubing.

• Drill a 1" hole in the center of one of the pieces of Plexiglas.

• Sand the ends of the acrylic tubing and the edges of the Plexiglas smooth, and attach the pieces of Plexiglas to either end of the acrylic tubing with acrylic cement so that the holes are toward the top.

• Insert the rubber grommets into the two holes in the acrylic tubing that are the farthest apart.

• Thread the cut nozzle into the coupler, thread the coupler onto the nipple, and insert the nipple into one of the grommets in the acrylic tube. Insert the screen into the bowl.

• Insert one end of the vinyl hose about ½" into the other grommet, and thread the pyramid knob (if using) onto the other end of the hose.

• Insert the stopper into the hole in the Plexiglas.

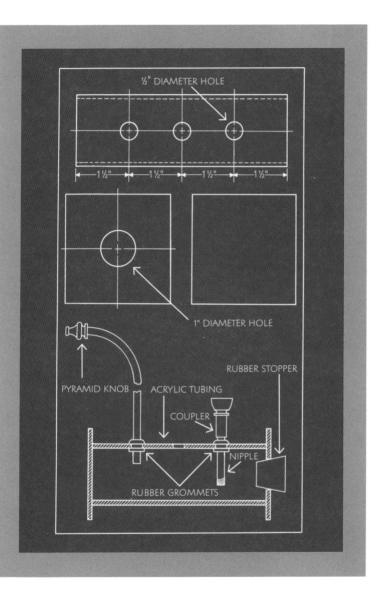

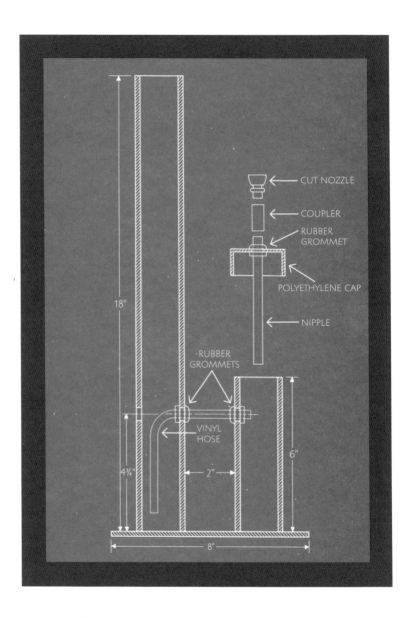

CUT NOZZLE

COUPLER

RUBBER GROMMET

POLYETHYLENE CAP

NIPPLE

RUBBER GROMMETS

VINYL HOSE

18"

4¾"

6"

2"

8"

DUAL-CHAMBER BONG

Materials and Supplies

One 2' length of 2" OD acrylic tubing

One 4" × 8" piece of ⅛"-thick Plexiglas

Acrylic cement

Three ⅜" ID × ⅝" OD rubber grommets

One 8" length of ¼" ID × ⅜" OD flexible vinyl hose

One 2" ID polyethylene cap

One ⅜" or ¼" F × ⅛" M brass cut nozzle

One ⅛" F brass coupler

One 5" × ⅛" M brass nipple

Screen (an aerator screen cut to fit the bowl, or an appropriately sized screen purchased from a smoke shop)

Tools

Drill and ½" drill bit (with a 60-degree or bullet-point tip)

Sandpaper

Directions

• Cut the acrylic tubing into one piece 6" long, and one piece 18" long.

• Drill two ½" holes on opposite sides of the longer piece of acrylic tubing, about 4¾" up from the bottom. Drill one ½" hole in the shorter piece of tubing, about 4¾" up from the bottom.

• Sand the ends of the acrylic tubing and the edges of the Plexiglas smooth.

(continued)

• Cement the two pieces of acrylic tubing onto the Plexiglas base 2" apart from each other and so that the hole in the shorter piece and the holes in the longer piece are all in line.

• Insert one grommet into the hole in the shorter piece of acrylic tubing, and another into the hole opposite it in the longer piece of acrylic tubing. Insert one end of the hose about ½" into the grommet in the shorter piece of acrylic tubing, and insert the other end of the hose about 4" into the grommet in the taller piece of acrylic tubing, angling it toward the bottom.

• Drill a ½" hole in the top of the polyethylene cap, and insert a rubber grommet into the hole. Thread the cut nozzle into the coupler, and thread the coupler onto the nipple. Insert the nipple into the grommet in the polyethylene cap, and place the cap on the shorter piece of acrylic tubing. Insert the screen into the bowl.

Note: To use, simply fill the smaller cylinder with about 4" of water, or fill the smaller cylinder with about 4" of hot water and the taller cylinder with an equal amount of ice water.

HYBRID

Materials and Supplies

One 2' length of 2" OD acrylic tubing

Three 4" × 4" pieces of ⅛"-thick Plexiglas

Acrylic cement

Three ⅜" ID × ⅝" OD rubber grommets

One ⅜" or ¼" F × ⅛" M brass cut nozzle

One ⅛" F brass coupler

One 2" × ⅛" M brass nipple

Screen (an aerator screen cut to fit the bowl, or an appropriately sized screen purchased from a smoke shop)

One 12" length of ¼" ID × ⅜" OD flexible vinyl hose

One 1" rubber stopper

Tools

Drill and ½" drill bit (with a 60-degree or bullet-point tip)

1" boring bit

Sandpaper

Directions

• Cut the acrylic tubing into one piece 6" long, and one piece 18" long.

• Drill two ½" holes on opposite sides of the long piece of acrylic tubing about 4¾" up from the bottom.

• Drill two ½" holes about 3" apart from each other on one side of the shorter piece of tubing.

(continued)

• Drill a 1" hole in the center of one of the pieces of Plexiglas.

• Sand the ends of the acrylic tubing and the edges of the Plexiglas smooth.

• Cement the longer piece of acrylic tubing onto one of the pieces of Plexiglas without a hole.

• Cement pieces of Plexiglas, one with a hole and one without, to each end of the shorter piece of acrylic tubing so that the holes in the tubing are facing up.

• Insert rubber grommets into the two holes in the shorter piece of acrylic tubing, and into one of the holes in the longer piece of acrylic tubing.

• Thread the cut nozzle into the coupler, thread the coupler onto the nipple, and insert the nipple into the grommet at one end of the shorter piece of acrylic tubing. Insert the screen into the bowl.

• Insert one end of the hose about ½" into the other grommet in the short piece of acrylic tubing, and insert the other end of the hose about 4" into the grommet in the longer piece of acrylic tubing, angling it downward.

• Insert the stopper into the hole in the piece of Plexiglas.

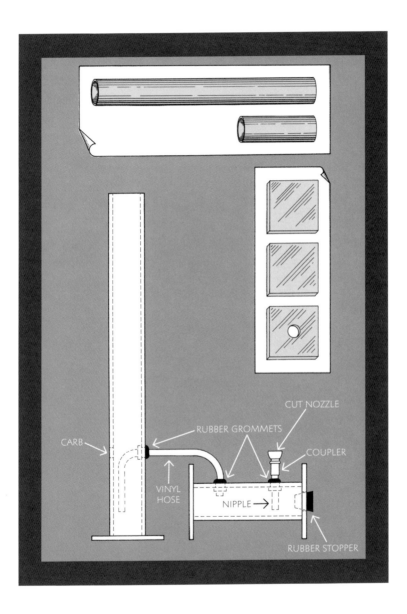

CUT NOZZLE

COUPLER

RUBBER GROMMETS

CARB

VINYL HOSE

NIPPLE →

RUBBER STOPPER

69

TANDEM BONG

Materials

One 3' length of 2" OD × 1¾" ID acrylic tubing

One 4" × 12" piece of ¼"-thick Plexiglas

Acrylic cement

One 2" ID polyethylene cap

Five ⅜" ID × ⅝" OD rubber grommets

One ⅜" or ¼" F × ⅛" M brass cut nozzle

One ⅛" F brass coupler

One 5" × ⅛" M brass nipple

Screen (an aerator screen cut to fit the bowl, or an appropriately sized screen purchased from a smoke shop)

One 2' length of ¼" ID × ⅜" OD flexible vinyl hose

Tools

Drill and ½" drill bit (with a 60-degree or bullet-point tip)

Sandpaper

Directions

• Cut one piece of acrylic tubing 6" long, and cut the remaining piece in half at a slight angle, 22.5 degrees or less.

• Drill two ½" holes on opposite sides of the shorter piece of acrylic tubing, about 4¾" up from the bottom of the tube. Drill two ½" holes on opposite sides of each of the longer pieces of tubing, about 4¾" up from the bottom.

• Sand the ends of the acrylic tubing and the edges of the Plexiglas smooth.

(continued)

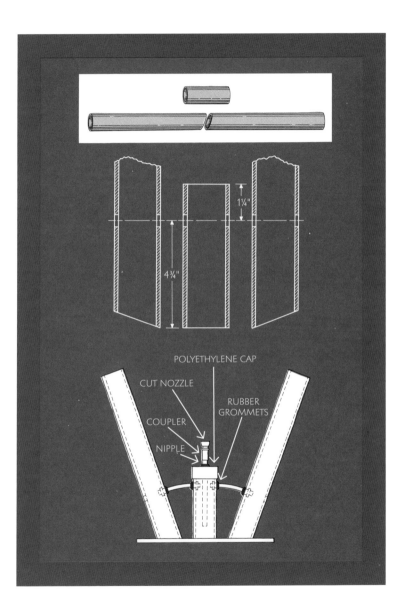

1¼"

4¾"

POLYETHYLENE CAP

CUT NOZZLE

COUPLER

RUBBER
GROMMETS

NIPPLE

• Cement the shorter piece of acrylic tubing onto the center of the Plexiglas base, and cement the longer pieces on opposite ends of the Plexiglas, angled away from each other. The holes on all the pieces should line up with each other.

• Drill a ½" hole in the center of the polyethylene cap, and insert a grommet into the hole. Thread the cut nozzle into the coupler, and thread the coupler onto the nipple. Insert the nipple into the rubber grommet, and place the cap on the shorter piece of acrylic tubing. Insert the screen into the bowl.

• Insert grommets into the two holes in the shorter piece of acrylic tubing, and the two holes opposite them in each of the long pieces of acrylic tubing.

• Cut the vinyl hose in half. Insert one end of each piece of hose about ½" into the grommets in the shorter piece of acrylic tubing. Insert the other ends of the hose about 4" into the rubber grommets in the taller pieces of acrylic tubing, angling them downward.

Note: To use, simply fill the smaller cylinder with about 4" of water, or fill the smaller cylinder with about 4" of hot water, and the taller cylinders with an equal amount of ice water.

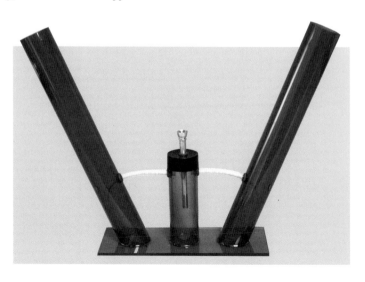

72

UMBILICAL BONG

Materials and Supplies

One 2' length of 2" OD acrylic tubing

One 6" × 6" piece of ⅛"-thick Plexiglas

Acrylic cement

Two 2" ID polyethylene caps

Three ⅜" ID × ⅝" OD rubber grommets

One ⅜" or ¼" F × ⅛" M brass cut nozzle

One ⅛" F brass coupler

One 5" × ⅛" M brass nipple

Screen (an aerator screen cut to fit the bowl, or an appropriately sized screen purchased from a smoke shop)

One 2' length of ¼" ID × ⅜" OD flexible vinyl hose

Tools

Drill and ½" drill bit (with a 60-degree or bullet-point tip)

Sandpaper

(continued)

Directions

• Cut the acrylic tubing into one piece 6" long, and one piece 18" long.

• Drill one ½" hole in the shorter piece of acrylic tubing about 1¼" down from the top, and drill one ½" hole in the longer piece of acrylic tubing about 2" in from one end.

• Sand the ends of the acrylic tubing and the edges of the Plexiglas smooth, and cement the shorter piece of acrylic tubing onto the center of the Plexiglas base.

• Drill one ½" hole in the center of each of the polyethylene caps, and insert rubber grommets into the holes.

• Thread the cut nozzle into the coupler, and thread the coupler onto the nipple. Insert the nipple into the grommet in one of the polyethylene caps, and place the cap with the stem and bowl on the shorter piece of acrylic tubing. Insert the screen into the bowl. Place the other cap on the end of the longer piece of acrylic tubing nearest the hole.

• Insert the remaining grommet into one of the holes in the shorter piece of acrylic tubing. Connect the longer piece to the shorter piece by inserting one end of the vinyl hose about ½" into the rubber grommets on the end of the longer piece and about 4" into the side of the shorter piece, angling it downward.

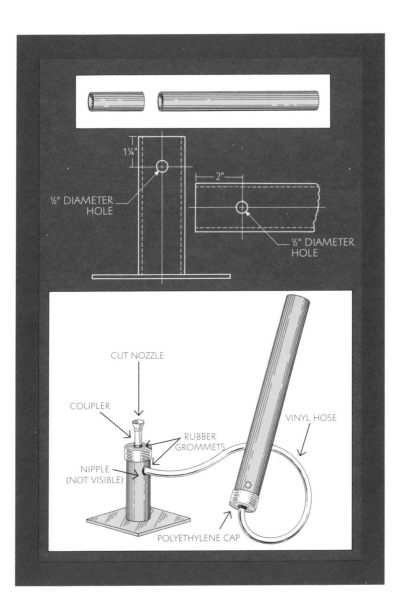

1¼"

½" DIAMETER
HOLE

2"

½" DIAMETER
HOLE

CUT NOZZLE

COUPLER

RUBBER
GROMMETS

NIPPLE
(NOT VISIBLE)

VINYL HOSE

POLYETHYLENE CAP

ACRYLIC STEAMROLLER

Materials and Supplies

One 12" length of 2" OD × 1¾" ID acrylic tubing

One ⅜" ID × ⅝" OD rubber grommet

One ⅜" or ¼" F × ⅛" M brass cut nozzle

One ⅛" F brass coupler

One 2" × ⅛" M brass nipple

Screen (an aerator screen cut to fit the bowl, or an appropriately sized screen purchased from a smoke shop)

Tools

Drill and ½" drill bit (with a 60-degree or bullet-point tip)

Sandpaper

Directions

• Drill one ½" hole in the acrylic tubing about 3" in from one end.

• Sand the ends of the acrylic tubing smooth.

• Insert the rubber grommet into the hole in the acrylic tubing. Thread the cut nozzle into the coupler, thread the coupler onto the nipple, and insert the nipple into the grommet. Insert the screen into the bowl.

Note: To use, cover the end of the tube with one hand, and remove when the tube is full to release the smoke.

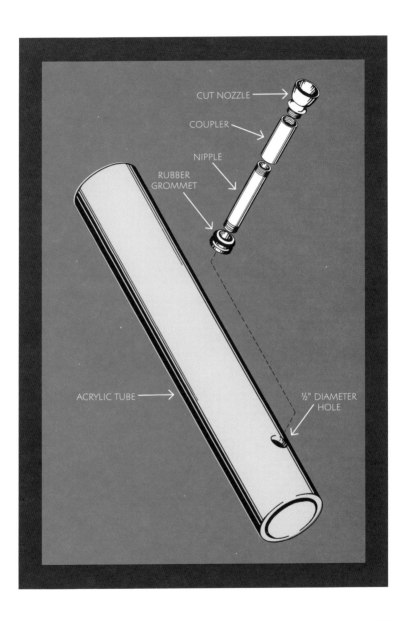

CUT NOZZLE

COUPLER

NIPPLE

RUBBER
GROMMET

ACRYLIC TUBE

½" DIAMETER
HOLE

GETTING CREATIVE

By now it should be obvious that bongs, pipes, and hookahs are such simple devices that you can make them from almost anything. Additionally, smoking devices made from found objects can be both impressive and expressive. They can be conversation pieces themselves, or they can be cleverly disguised as everyday objects. The projects in this section will show you how to turn ordinary objects, like snow globes or rubber ducks, into extraordinary bongs and hookahs.

When making a bong, hookah, or pipe using a found object, you may also wish to use parts that will help give your creation a more finished look. It's good to know that most smoke shops also sell bong bowl-and-stem assemblies, pipe bowls, and mouthpieces individually, in addition to the usual fully assembled, premade bongs and pipes. Though pieces of plumbing and lamp hardware may work perfectly well, parts obtained from smoke shops usually look better. Most parts are made of either brass or aluminum and come in a variety of finishes and colors. A smoke shop is also a reliable source for screens of almost any size, rubber grommets, and stoppers. Before long you may even find yourself trying to make a bong out of everything you see, or at least thinking about how you might go about it.

HONEY-BEAR BONG

Materials and Supplies

One empty plastic bear-shaped honey container

One ⅜" ID × ⅝" OD rubber grommet

One ⅜" or ¼" F × ⅛" M brass cut nozzle

One ⅛" F brass coupler

One 2" × ⅛" M brass nipple

Screen (an aerator screen cut to fit the bowl, or an appropriately sized screen purchased from a smoke shop)

Tools

X-Acto knife, or similar sharp, pointy instrument

Directions

• Using the knife, cut one ½" hole in the back of the honey bear's head, and one in the honey bear's chest.

• Insert the rubber grommet into the hole in the honey bear's chest. Thread the cut nozzle into the coupler, thread the coupler onto the nipple, and insert the nipple into the grommet in the honey bear's chest. Insert the screen into the bowl.

CUT NOZZLE

COUPLER

NIPPLE

RUBBER
GROMMET

RUBBER DUCK HOOKAH

Materials and Supplies

One large rubber duck (the bigger, the better)

Two ⅜" ID × ⅝" OD rubber grommets

One ⅜" or ¼" F × ⅛" M brass cut nozzle

One ⅛" F brass coupler

One ⅛" M brass nipple (the length will depend on the size of the rubber duck)

Screen (an aerator screen cut to fit the bowl, or an appropriately sized screen purchased from a smoke shop)

One 12" length of ¼" ID × ⅜" OD flexible vinyl hose

One ⅛" F brass pyramid knob with a hole for a beaded chain (optional)

Tools

X-Acto knife, or similar sharp, pointy instrument

Drill and ½" drill bit (optional)

Directions

• Cut or drill one ½" hole in the rubber duck's forehead, and one in the back of the rubber duck's head. Make another ½" hole in the rubber duck's rear end for a carb.

• Insert the two rubber grommets into the holes in the rubber duck's forehead and the back of its head.

• Thread the cut nozzle into the coupler, thread the coupler onto the nipple, and insert the nipple into the grommet in the rubber duck's forehead. Insert the screen into the bowl.

• Insert one end of the vinyl hose about 1" into the grommet in the back of the rubber duck's head, and thread the pyramid knob (if using) onto the other end of the hose.

Note: If there is a squeaking device in the bottom of the rubber duck, it must be plugged to avoid leakage. How you plug it will depend on the kind of squeaking device, the size of the hole, and what you have readily available. Silicone caulk or an appropriate size cork are just a couple of possibilities.

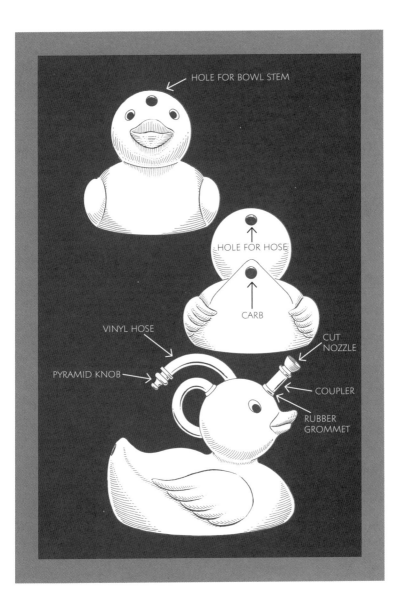

83

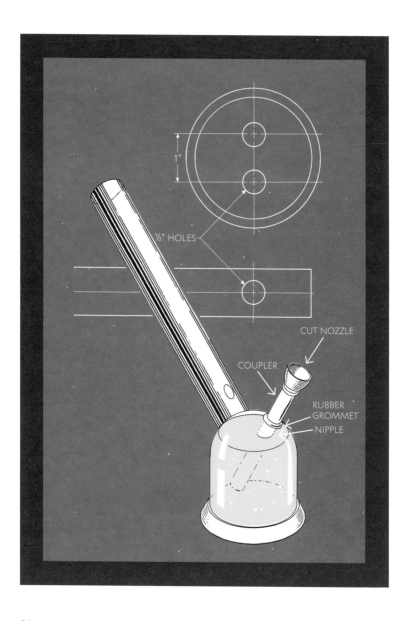

1" HOLES

½" HOLES

CUT NOZZLE

COUPLER

RUBBER
GROMMET

NIPPLE

SNOW GLOBE BONG

Materials and Supplies

One large plastic snow globe (the bigger, the better)

One 12" length of 1" OD acrylic tubing

Acrylic cement

One ⅜" or ¼" F × ⅛" M brass cut nozzle

One ⅛" F brass coupler

One ⅛" M brass nipple (the length depends on the size of the snow globe)

One ⅜" ID × ⅝" OD rubber grommet

Screen (an aerator screen cut to fit the bowl, or an appropriately sized screen purchased from a smoke shop)

Glitter

Tools

Drill and ½" drill bit (with a 60-degree or bullet-point tip)

Directions

• Drill ½" holes in the front and back of the snow globe near the top, and drain out the liquid. Be sure that the holes are centered and at least 1" apart. *Note: Because snow globes are typically made of low-grade plastic, which tends to be extremely brittle, use caution when drilling to avoid breaking the globe. It is best to start the holes with a smaller drill bit, and work your way up to the larger bit.*

• Drill a ½" hole in the lower part of the acrylic tube for a carb, and attach the tube to the snow globe with acrylic cement, centering it over the hole in the back side of the globe.

• Thread the cut nozzle into the coupler, and thread the coupler onto the nipple. Insert the rubber grommet into the hole in the front of the snow globe, and insert the nipple into the grommet. Insert the screen into the bowl.

Note: To achieve a "snow" effect, add glitter to the water when using.

COCONUT BONG

Materials and Supplies

One large coconut

One sturdy plastic beverage straw, such as a Krazy Straw

One ¼" HB × ¼" F brass hose barb–to–pipe adapter

One 6" length of ¼" ID × ⅜" OD flexible vinyl hose

Screen (an aerator screen cut to fit the bowl, or an appropriately sized screen purchased from a smoke shop)

One paper cocktail umbrella

One small cork (small enough to fit into a ⅜" hole)

Tools

Drill, ⅜" drill bit, and ¼" drill bit (actual sizes depend on the outside diameter of the straw to be used)

Directions

• Drill one ¼" hole in one of the dimples in the top of the coconut, and one ⅜" hole in each of the other two dimples.

• Cut the lower part of the straw so that it is only slightly longer than the thickness of the coconut, and insert it into the ¼" hole.

• Insert the hose barb into one end of the hose, and insert the other end of the hose into one of the ⅜" holes in the coconut. Insert the screen into the bowl.

• Insert the paper cocktail umbrella pick into the cork, and insert the cork into the other ⅜" hole in the coconut. When using, remove the cork to release the smoke.

Note: The liquid inside the coconut may be used in place of water.

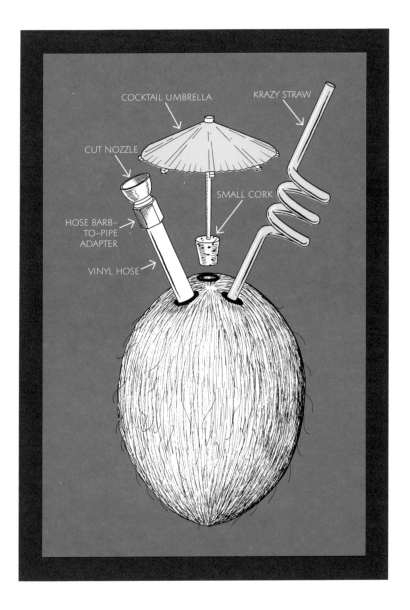

COCKTAIL UMBRELLA

KRAZY STRAW

CUT NOZZLE

HOSE BARB–
TO–PIPE
ADAPTER

SMALL CORK

VINYL HOSE

87

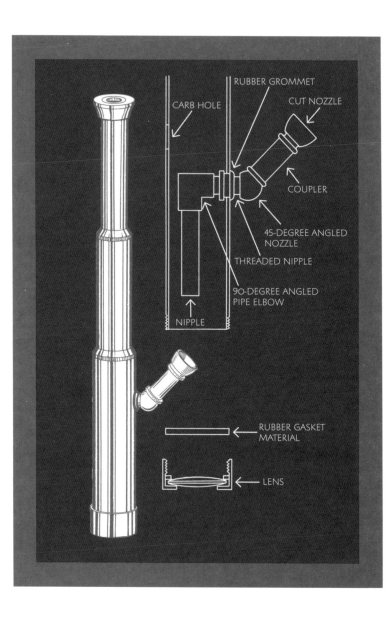

RUBBER GROMMET

CUT NOZZLE

CARB HOLE

COUPLER

45-DEGREE ANGLED NOZZLE

THREADED NIPPLE

90-DEGREE ANGLED PIPE ELBOW

NIPPLE

RUBBER GASKET MATERIAL

LENS

SPYGLASS BONG

Materials

One spyglass or telescope

One ⅜" ID × ⅝" OD rubber grommet

One 2" × ⅛" M brass nipple

One ⅛" F × ⅛" F 90-degree-angle brass pipe elbow

One 1" × ⅛" M brass nipple

One ⅜" or ¼" F × ⅛" M brass cut nozzle

One ⅛" coupler

One ⅛" F × ⅛" M 45-degree-angle brass nozzle

Screen (an aerator screen cut to fit the bowl, or an appropriately sized screen purchased from a smoke shop)

Rubber gasket material

Tools

Drill and ½" drill bit

Directions

• Remove all lenses from the telescope or spyglass so that you are left with an unobstructed telescoping tube.

• Drill a ½" hole on one side of the largest part of the spyglass or telescope about 3" in from the lens end for the stem and bowl, and drill another ½" hole on the opposite side about 4" in from the lens end for the carb.

• Insert the rubber grommet into the lower hole. Thread the 2" nipple into one side of the 90-degree-angle pipe elbow. Insert the 1" nipple into the grommet, and thread it into the other side of the elbow on the inside of the spyglass or telescope. Thread the cut nozzle into the coupler, and thread the coupler onto the 45-degree-angle nozzle. Thread the 45-degree-angle nozzle into the nipple on the outside of the spyglass or telescope. Insert the screen into the bowl.

• Cut a piece of gasket material to fit inside the large lens ring, and thread it back onto the large end of the telescope.

• Remove the lens from the eyepiece ring, and thread the eyepiece back onto the small end of the telescope.

TEAPOT BONG

Materials and Supplies

One small, lightweight, metal teapot (with a removable knob and a handle that is either mounted on the side of the pot or hinged so that it is not always directly above the lid)

One nickel-chrome pipe bowl and lid, such as the kind found at a smoke shop (it should more or less match the teapot)

One ⅛" F brass coupler

⅛" M brass nipple (the length will depend on the size of the teapot)

Screen (an aerator screen cut to fit the bowl, or an appropriately sized screen purchased from a smoke shop)

Tools

Drill and ⅜" drill bit

Directions

• Unscrew and remove the knob from the lid of the teapot and enlarge the hole to ⅜". Enlarge the hole of the existing vent if there is one, for the carb.

• Thread the pipe bowl and lid into the outside of the lid of the teapot, thread the coupler onto the bowl on the inside of the lid of the teapot, and thread the nipple into the coupler. Insert the screen into the bowl.

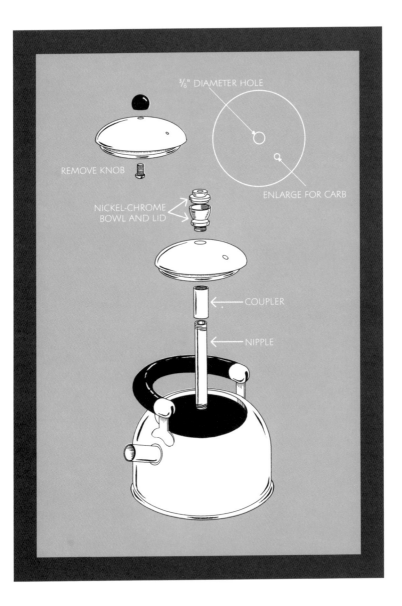

REMOVE KNOB

³⁄₈" DIAMETER HOLE

ENLARGE FOR CARB

NICKEL-CHROME
BOWL AND LID

COUPLER

NIPPLE

91

BOOK STASH-BOX

Materials and Supplies

One large hardcover book, such as a dictionary

Book board or heavy cardboard (the amount will depend on the size of the book)

Glue

Plain white paper

Tools

X-Acto knife, or similar sharp, pointy instrument

Ruler

Disposable foam brush, about 2" wide

Directions

• Remove the pages of the book from the cover by carefully cutting along the binding with the knife.

• Measure the stack of pages with the ruler and, using the book board and glue, make a box with four sides and a bottom that is the same finished size as the stack of pages.

• Cover the book board with the plain white paper using the brush and glue.

• Glue the bottom of the box to the inside of the back cover of the book.

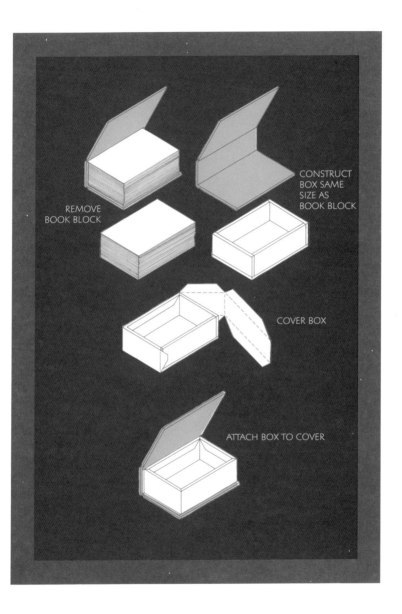

REMOVE
BOOK BLOCK

CONSTRUCT
BOX SAME
SIZE AS
BOOK BLOCK

COVER BOX

ATTACH BOX TO COVER

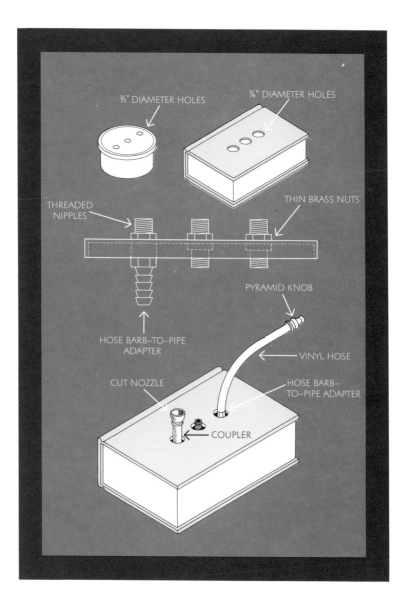

⅜" DIAMETER HOLES

¾" DIAMETER HOLES

THREADED NIPPLES

THIN BRASS NUTS

PYRAMID KNOB

HOSE BARB–TO–PIPE ADAPTER

VINYL HOSE

CUT NOZZLE

HOSE BARB–TO–PIPE ADAPTER

COUPLER

BOOK HOOKAH

Materials

One large hardcover book, such as a dictionary

One large piece of book board or heavy cardboard (size will depend on the size of the book)

Plain white paper

Glue

One empty plastic food-storage container (slightly shallower than the thickness of the book)

Three 1" × ⅛" threaded nipples

Five ⅛" thin brass nuts

Two ¼" HB × ⅛" F brass hose barb–to–pipe adapters

One ⅜" or ¼" F × ⅛" M brass cut nozzle

One ⅛" coupler

Screen (an aerator screen cut to fit the bowl, or an appropriately sized screen purchased from a smoke shop)

One 1" length of ¼" ID × ⅜" OD flexible vinyl hose

One small brass pyramid knob with a hole for a beaded chain (optional)

Tools

X-Acto knife, or similar sharp, pointy instrument

Disposable foam brush, about 2" wide

Drill and ⅜" drill bit

Directions

• Follow the procedure for the Book Stash-Box (page 92).

• Cut three ⅜" holes in the lid of the plastic container, and drill three corresponding ¾" holes in the front cover of the book.

• Attach the three threaded nipples to the lid of the plastic container with the brass nuts, and one of the hose barb–to–pipe adapters as shown.

• Fill the container approximately two-thirds full of water. Place the lid on the container, and place the container inside the book box. Align the holes in the front cover of the book with the nipples, and close the cover.

• Thread the cut nozzle into the coupler, and thread the coupler onto one of the nipples. Insert the screen into the bowl. Insert the other hose barb–to–pipe adapter into one end of the hose, and thread the adapter onto one of the other nipples. Thread a pyramid knob (if using) onto the other end of the hose.

• When not in use, disassemble and store the pieces inside the box. A paper jacket may be used to mask the holes in the cover of the book.

From the Past to the Present

Smoking devices have come a long way from their humble origins. This section will explain how to make two smoking devices from opposite ends of the spectrum: first, a bamboo bong, much like those first encountered in Vietnam in the late '60s and early '70s, and last, the vaporizer of today.

Making a bong from bamboo may prove harder than you might think, since bamboo is less common here than it is throughout most of Asia. It is possible to find bamboo at some garden-supply stores, though, and well worth the effort it might take. Simplicity often belies richness, and you may find that it is easy to appreciate the technological advances of the day through understanding what they evolved from. Making and using an actual bamboo bong can help put history into perspective.

Meanwhile, making and using a vaporizer will help you appreciate how much smoking devices have evolved. Vaporizers are considerably more high-tech than their ancestors. They use electricity rather than the flame from a match or a lighter to get things burning, and they do not get quite as hot. Because of this, vaporizers are said to burn cleaner and more efficiently, releasing fewer harmful emissions. While not nearly as simple as constructing an average bong, it is possible to make a vaporizer with a few easily obtainable materials and supplies. There are, of course, certain dangers inherent in any device that uses electricity. However, if the instructions are followed carefully, your vaporizer will be as safe as can be.

Somewhere between the time-tested *thuoc lao* pipe and the ultra-efficient vaporizer, there is probably a bong, pipe, or hookah for everyone and every occasion. If you still haven't found the one that's right for you, then invent your own!

A BAMBOO BONG,
OR VIETNAMESE *THUOC LAO* PIPE

Materials and Supplies

One long section of dry bamboo approximately 2" in diameter (If it is necessary to cut a section of bamboo from a longer stalk, cut approximately ½" below a "knuckle.")

One 3" long piece of ½" hardwood dowel

One 1" long piece of 1" hardwood dowel

Tools

Saw

Drill and ⅛" through ½" drill bits

½" boring bit

Sandpaper

Directions

• Drill a hole for the stem 3" from the bottom of the section of bamboo by making a shallow starter hole with the ⅛" drill bit. Once the hole is started, drill the rest of the way through with the bit angled toward the bottom of the section of bamboo. Enlarge the hole by moving up to the next largest drill bit (³⁄₁₆"), again angling toward the bottom. Continue to enlarge the hole at an angle until it is ½" in diameter.

Be careful! Dry bamboo can be brittle and will splinter easily.

• Drill a (straight) ½" hole 4" from the bottom on the opposite side of the bamboo for a carb, if desired. (A traditional Vietnamese *thuoc lao* pipe does not have a carb. When the contents of the bowl have been burned, a short, sharp breath is blown back into the pipe to clear the bowl, which then serves as the carb, and then the smoke in the pipe is inhaled. This may take practice.)

• Drill a ⅛" hole all the way through the center of the ½" dowel.

• Using the boring bit, drill a ½" diameter hole about halfway through one side of the 1" dowel, then drill from the other side of the dowel until the boring bit breaks through to the other hole.

• Sand all rough edges smooth.

• Insert one end of the ½" dowel into the 1" dowel, and insert the other end of the ½" dowel into the angled hole in the section of bamboo.

Note: Soaking the thuoc lao *pipe before its first use will cause the bamboo and hardwood to swell, helping prevent leaks.*

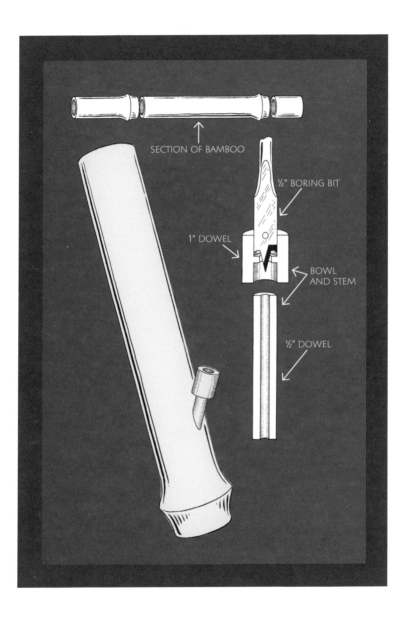

SECTION OF BAMBOO

½" BORING BIT

1" DOWEL

BOWL AND STEM

½" DOWEL

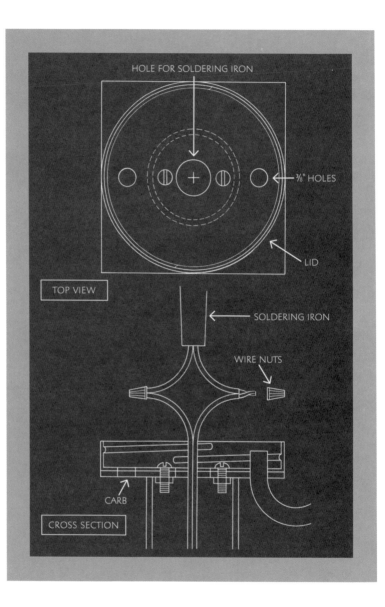

HOLE FOR SOLDERING IRON

⅜" HOLES

LID

TOP VIEW

SOLDERING IRON

WIRE NUTS

CARB

CROSS SECTION

VAPORIZER

Materials and Supplies

One soldering iron (25 watt, or less, with removable soldering tip)

One large, wide-mouth jar (a 32-ounce mayonnaise jar with a plastic lid will work well)

One 4" × 4" piece of ¼"-thick Plexiglas

Two small machine screws, ½" to ¾" long with corresponding nuts

One 6" length of 2" OD × 1¾" ID acrylic tubing

One 6" × 6" piece of ¼"-thick Plexiglas

Acrylic cement

Two small-gauge wire nuts (gray or blue)

One ¾" brass nut cap, or similar, to be used as a bowl

One small brass round-head machine screw (Size depends on soldering iron. It should fit into the end of the iron, in place of the soldering tip. This will be used to attach the nut cap to the top of the soldering iron.)

One 12" length of ¼" ID × ⅜" OD flexible vinyl hose

One ⅛" F brass pyramid knob with a hole for a beaded chain (optional)

Tools

Drill and ⅜" drill bit (with a 60-degree or bullet-point tip) and small drill bit (size will depend on the size of the screws used to attach the lid of the jar to the Plexiglas)

Boring bit (size depends on the diameter of the handle of the soldering iron)

Sandpaper

Directions

Note: The following directions are intended to serve as guidelines. Because most soldering irons are similar in many respects, but different in others, much will depend on the soldering iron used for this project.

• Cut the electrical cord of the soldering iron about 4" from the end of the handle.

• Using the drill and boring bit, drill a hole in the center of the lid of the jar and the 4" × 4" piece of Plexiglas. The hole should be large enough to insert the bottom of the handle of the soldering iron into, but not so

(continued)

large that the soldering iron will fall through it.

• Attach the lid of the jar and the 4" × 4" piece of Plexiglas to each other with the two small machine screws and nuts. These will then eventually be attached to the end of the acrylic tubing, so it is important to make sure that the screws and nuts will fit inside the tubing.

• Drill a ⅜" hole in the piece of acrylic tubing about 1" up from the bottom.

• Sand the edges of the Plexiglas and the ends of the acrylic tubing smooth, and attach the 4" × 4" piece of Plexiglas and lid to the top of the acrylic tubing with acrylic cement. Attach the bottom of the acrylic tubing to the center of the 6" × 6" piece of Plexiglas, and allow the cement to dry according to directions on its package before proceeding.

• After the cement has dried completely, drill two ⅜" diameter holes through the lid and 4" × 4" piece of Plexiglas in the area between the walls of the lid and the acrylic tubing.

• Feed the end of the soldering iron's electrical cord (the end that is still attached to the plug) through the hole in the bottom of the acrylic tubing, then through the hole in the lid and 4" × 4" piece of Plexiglas. Once through, split the ends of both the cord attached to the plug and the soldering iron approximately 1"–2", then strip the ends of all four wires

approximately ¼". Re-attach the two pieces of electrical cord by twisting the ends together and threading the wire nuts onto the exposed wire.

• Once the electrical cord has been re-attached, pull the cord back through the holes so that the handle of the soldering iron now rests in the hole in the lid and 4" × 4" piece of Plexiglas.

• Remove the soldering tip from the soldering iron. Drill a hole in the center of the nut cap just big enough for the brass round-head screw to pass through, and thread the screw into the tip of the soldering iron. This will be the bowl.

• Insert one end of the vinyl hose into one of the ⅜" holes in the lid and 4" × 4" piece of Plexiglas, and thread the pyramid knob (if using) onto the other end of the vinyl hose.

Note: To use the vaporizer, fill the bowl, screw the jar into its lid, and plug the soldering iron into an electrical outlet. You will know the vaporizer has reached the correct temperature, which can take several minutes, when a white cloud begins to appear inside the chamber. This means the contents of the bowl have begun to vaporize. As soon as the contents of the bowl begin to vaporize, unplug the soldering iron to prevent overheating. The vapor in the chamber is ready to be inhaled. The carb hole makes clearing the chamber easier, but it need not be covered to prevent the vapor from escaping the chamber, as little vapor is likely to escape.

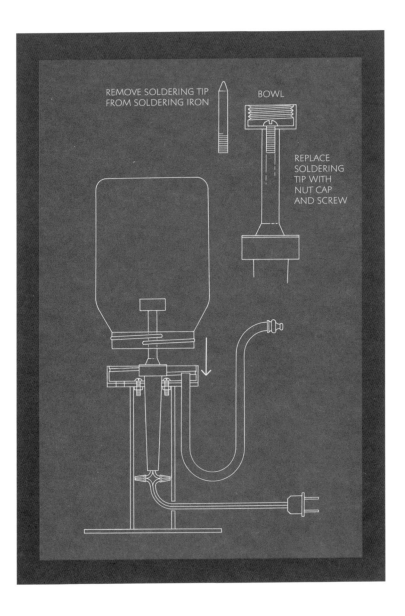

REMOVE SOLDERING TIP FROM SOLDERING IRON

BOWL

REPLACE SOLDERING TIP WITH NUT CAP AND SCREW

103

GLOSSARY

ABS/PVC: ABS and PVC are plastic compounds used to make pipes and fittings for plumbing and irrigation. ABS and PVC plastic pipe come in a few different diameters that work well for bongs, and are often sold in lengths as short as four feet. There are also assorted plastic joints and fittings available for ABS and PVC pipe.

Acrylic cement: Acrylic cement is a clear, solvent-type adhesive that is specifically formulated for acrylic and Plexiglas. It literally welds pieces of plastic together.

Angled nozzles: Nozzles of different angles —90 and 45 degrees, for example—can be used to turn pipe and bong stems in a particular direction.

Bowl: The bowl is the container in which the material that is to be burned and smoked is contained.

Carb: The word *carb* is likely derived from the word *carburetor*. A carb increases the amount of air that can enter a smoking device by providing a point of entry other than the relatively small and constricted opening in the bottom of the bowl. The use of a carb makes clearing the smoke-filled chamber easier.

Compression nut–to–pipe adapter: Bowls and stems can be made using a compression nut–to–pipe adapter and a length of brass tubing. A good standard combination is a ¼"

compression nut to a ¼" F pipe adapter, with ¼" OD brass tubing. This type of bowl and stem requires some form of seal to prevent leaks.

Coupler: A coupler is a fitting that joins two things together. It is threaded on the inside, and can be used to connect a male threaded pipe to a male threaded fitting, for example.

Cut nozzle: Cut nozzles are found in the lighting section of the hardware store or in stores that specialize in lamps and lighting. The standard size used for bowls is ⅜" F × ⅛" M. (The next smallest size, ¼" F × ⅛" M, also works well.)

Elbow: In hardware terminology, an elbow is a fitting used to join sections of pipe, tubing, or other fittings at a particular angle, usually 90 or 45 degrees.

Flexible vinyl hose: Flexible vinyl hose can be used for the stem of a bong, or to connect a mouthpiece to a hookah. Flexible vinyl hose is usually sold by the linear foot, and can be found at hardware stores as well as aquarium-supply shops. The sizes of the outside and inside diameters are given as OD and ID, respectively. The OD will determine the size of the hole the hose will fit into, and ID will determine the size of the fitting that will fit into it. For example, a piece of ½" OD x ⅜" ID hose will fit into a ½" diameter hole, and a

³⁄₈" hose barb will fit into it. When inserted snugly into the appropriate diameter hole, flexible vinyl hose will provide a relatively leak-proof seal without the use of a rubber grommet.

Hose barb–to–pipe adapter: Just as the name implies, hose barb–to–pipe adapters can join flexible hose to threaded pipe. The simplest way to make a bowl and stem for a bong is to insert a brass hose barb–to–pipe adapter into a piece of flexible vinyl hose. Hose barb–to–pipe adapters are available in both male and female threading.

Male/female: *Male* and *female* indicate whether the threads are on the outside or inside of a pipe or fitting. Male pipes and fittings are threaded on the outside, meaning they get threaded into something. Female pipes and fittings are threaded on the inside, meaning that something is threaded into them. Male or female threading is usually indicated by either an *M* or an *F*. It may also appear as either *MIP* or *FIP.*

MIP/FIP: MIP stands for *male iron pipe.* FIP stands for *female iron pipe.* Iron pipe sizes are nominal, meaning they do not reflect the actual diameter of the pipe or fitting.

Nipple: In plumbing terminology, a "nipple" is a short length of pipe (12" long or less) that is threaded on both ends. These are useful for bong stems, as well as for pipes.

Plexiglas: Plexiglas is brand name, but used generically it refers to any translucent sheet acrylic.

Pyramid knob: The mouthpiece on most pipes is usually what is referred to as a small pyramid knob, with a hole for a beaded chain.

Rubber grommets: Rubber grommets may be found in either hardware stores or smoke shops. They provide a seal between a stem or hose and the body of a bong or hookah, helping to prevent leaks.

Screens: Screens are not required for use with store-bought bong bowls, as the inside diameter of the opening in the bottom of the bowl is usually very small and acts as a screen, and the water filters out anything else that might get through. Screens can be found in either hardware stores or smoke shops. In hardware stores, they are found in the plumbing department, and are referred to as aerator screens. They are usually sold in a variety of diameters, but larger screens can easily be cut down with a pair of scissors when a smaller screen is not readily available.

Stem: The stem connects the bowl to the body of a bong or hookah, or to the mouthpiece of a pipe.

Threaded nipple: Found in the lighting section of the hardware store or in stores that specialize in lamps and lighting, threaded nipples are similar to regular plumbing nipples, but they are threaded down their entire length.

INDEX

Randy Stratton is, among other things, an illustrator, bookbinder, and metalsmith. He has degrees in both art and motorcycle maintenance. He lives in San Francisco.